IT WASN'T MY TIME

To Jeff

Wayne White

IT WASN'T MY TIME

By Wayne W. White

ISBN 978-1-257-11257-9

Dedication

To my children, my grandchildren, my great grandchildren and all the generations to come. I want them to know my story and what my life was like during WWII and why our freedom is so precious.

Love, Grandpa Wayne

Introduction

I grew up in Tennessee, Illinois, a little town in the mid-west. I went to the high school in the next little town of Colchester and graduated in 1940. In 1942 I married my high school sweetheart Bette Jane Wayland. This is a story of my time in the United States Army Air Force during World War II. The memories have stayed with me over the years. The trauma of combat leaves a impression on ones mind. I experienced situations that were so full of fear, trauma, and emotion that they are difficult to put into words. No matter what direction my life has taken, this time as a member of the United States 15th Army Air Force remains significant and after over sixty years clear in my mind.

My children from time to time ask about the events that took place so many years ago. To my delight they seem interested.

Preface

It was a time when good and evil contended for the world! And we should all know, and the world should well know that without the United States contribution to the war, civilization as we know it, would not have survived.

But, thank God, not all our soldiers died. Millions of the 16 million who wore a uniform survived and some of them, including me, are still with us today. Because of our age, we are losing over a thousand WWII veterans every day. There are not many of us left to tell the stories. I was 20 years old then. It was a different time.

During those years we had no TVs yet or the internet or the cell phone, so as young people we didn't know a lot about other parts of the world. Most of us had never been away from home let alone be in a war plane bombing oil fields in another part of the world!

Americans were underestimated by the enemy. They thought we were lazy, soft, undisciplined, unprepared and none too smart. But our enemies then didn't understand the character of free men.

It reminds me of the a quote from John Kennedy:

"Let every nation know, whether it wishes us well or ill, that we shall pay any price....bear any burden..... meet any hardship..... support any friend.....oppose any foe to assure the survival and the success of liberty."

Once Americans have been wronged, or held in contempt, or attacked in peace, we citizens, just ordinary folks, become warriors. This is what we did in World War II.

The courage and sacrifice of Americans knew no bounds. Winston Churchill once said of us:

> *"The United States is like a gigantic boiler. Once the fire is lit under it, there is no limit to the power it can generate."*

I was then and am still proud to be an American.

Contents

Me & My Wife Bette

War in Europe was going hot and heavy. The United States could see the need to help England protect itself from Hitler's quest to rule the world.

BURLINGTON, IOWA

The United States needed to build ammunition plants around the country. One was planned at West Burlington, Iowa, which was fairly close to my hometown. Of course that meant work there for a lot of men and women. I like many others, went and took a job building this plant. After the plant was built I took a job as explosive powder man in one of the lines making anti-tank mines. I was the only man with a key to the powder house. When the workers needed powder I would get it for them. My hands became very yellow from handling the powder. I knew I would be going into the service someday soon. All young men of my age either enlisted or were drafted. I also knew that the yellow stain on my hands was from (Trinitrophenol Nitromine). I thought that this yellow stain on my hands would concern the doctor when he gave me a physical for the service. Well it didn't. When I was finally called to take a physical the first words the Doctor said was, "*you have been working with TNT.*" That just blew me out of the water. Ha Ha.

Where We Lived in Government Trailers at Ammo Plant in Burlington, Iowa

My wife Bette and I rented a government trailer that had been set up to house the extra help needed in this area. The kitchen stoves were gas. You had to pump them up before using them. It was nothing for them to blow up; maybe one a day. I worked there until I was sure I would be drafted into the service. I didn't want to be a foot soldier.

I wanted to fly in an airplane. So, on October 31, 1942, Bette drove me and a friend of mine, Harold Matthews, to Peoria where we enlisted in the Army Air Force. We were put on a train that very afternoon and sent to Chanute Field near St. Louis. There we received our clothes and our shots before being sent to our bases wherever that was to be.

BT13- Basic Training Flight Plane

PERIN FIELD, TEXAS

Harold and I were sent by train to Perin Field at Dennison and Sherman, Texas to get our basic training. I remember that this old train had wicker seats that were very uncomfortable. This was a training to teach you how to march, run miles and do calisthenics as well as take orders. Harold was older than me and due to his age was assigned there and remained at that base for the duration of the war.

They had BT13's at this base. These were basic training planes for all types of flight instruction. I met one kid who had failed his glider pilot test but was certified to pre-flight the BT13 training planes on base. He was knowledgeable enough to start a plane up and check the guages. It was a Saturday and most of the officers were gone. Just for kicks, this kid decided to taxi a plane around. He made a big mistake when he came to a corner. He turned the plane directly into another BT13! It bent the props and damaged the wing. This kid was just sweating bullets all weekend wondering what would happen when the CO (Commanding Officer) came back. He took a lot of teasing about what would happen too. The CO came back and they were to meet in an orderly room to discuss his fate. The CO said, "*I would have taken off and FLOWN the son-of-a-bitch if it had been me!*" That kid was so lucky. He had to go to work in the orderly room and that was it. Pretty understanding CO.

Perin Field Flight Formation Training

LOWRY FIELD, DENVER, COLORADO

I was then sent to Lowry Field at Denver Colorado for 3 months to take a course in Photography as a camera technician. This was an assignment, not a choice. I was not upset with this assignment, but I just wanted to be an Air Force Cadet and be able to fly in an airplane. My wife Bette, followed me there as well. The first night I went to town I met Johnny Kessler, a kid from my hometown and I was glad to see someone from home. I told him Bette was coming out tomorrow and we would meet at the USO at 6:00pm and all go out to dinner together. Bette got there, but no Johnny. I called to Fort Carson and found out he had been shipped out that day.

Lowry Field

United States Army

Air Forces Technical School

Be it known that

private Wayne M. White, 16075918

has satisfactorily completed the prescribed

photography

course of instruction at the Air Forces Technical School.

In testimony whereof and by virtue of vested authority I do confer upon him this

———DIPLOMA———

Given on this   3rd   day of April

in the year of our Lord one thousand nine hundred and forty-three

DIRECTOR, DEPARTMENT OF PHOTOGRAPHY

ALAMOGORDO, NEW MEXICO

After graduating from this course in Colorado, I was given orders to take nine men to Alamogordo, New Mexico for their next training. I was chosen to be a leader I suppose because the Commanders thought I was trustworthy and mature enough to handle the challenge. That was a responsibility I didn't much care for because that would mean we had to lay over in Kansas City, and I would be responsible for a bunch of how should I say, not yet disciplined young men. When we were ready to leave two of the soldiers did not show up. When I found them I told them when the next train was to leave and if they weren't there we were going on and they would be considered AWOL. I guess that scared them so they were there on time for the next departure. I was glad when I got their orders delivered and had that off my shoulders.

PX at Alamogordo, New Mexico

I was assigned to the photo lab in Alamogordo. My main job was to take pictures of the dignitaries as they landed at the field. This was quite a easy job for me. Bette came there and we rented a garage apartment at 1415 Indiana Ave. She got a job at the PX Commissary (Post Exchange) and worked there the whole time I was at Alamogordo. This was like a military grocery store. We would have quite a bit of time together. We spent many Sundays at White Sands. It was just mile after mile of gorgeous white sand. I had to spend some time at the barracks. I couldn't stay in our apartment all of the time. The barracks were pretty crude. The sand would blow and drift inside the doors. Dust was on everything. It was flying through the air. It was kind of hard to breathe.

WHITE SANDS

I was at Alamogordo about 3 or 4 months when I received orders to report to McCook, Nebraska to hook up with an overseas group. Bette took me to the train station. When I went in to see when I would be going, the train master said, *"hurry your train is about to pull out!"* I didn't even get to say good-bye to my wife. That was an awful feeling. I hated leaving her there. I don't know what she thought, but I know it was torture for both of us. There were no means of communication like today. I couldn't call her. I am sure that she cried all the way home.

When I arrived in Nebraska the men had their stuff packed so I didn't even get to unpack my duffel bags.

Trainees at Charleston, South Carolina

CHARLESTON, SOUTH CAROLINA

The very next day we were on a troop train for Charleston, South Carolina for our last training for overseas duty. I had applied for Air Force cadet training way back when I was in Texas but hadn't heard anything about my request and was sure hoping that notification would come soon. Once again Bette came on the train to be with me and again we got to spend quite a bit of time together. Transportation wasn't like it is now. Trains were a major means of travel.

We got to know and chum around with some other couples in the evenings. Albert Ross and his wife, Kit, (USAAF) from St. Petersburg, Florida and Casey Siwiks and his wife Edna (Coast Guard) from Alabama. Ross and I became especially close.

Cass & Edna Siwik and Me & Bette

One day Sgt. Ross, myself and another airman named Joe went to town in Charleston on a bus. We just went for kicks and to see the town. Because there was a shortage of gas, not many people could drive their cars. Therefore, the buses were always really full. When we got on a bus that was almost full we went toward the back to find a seat. Ross and Joe set in the next to last seat and I took a seat in the back row. At the next bus stop there was a very old little black lady that got on the bus and had to come to the back. I got up and gave her my seat. I am sorry to say that not many people would have done something like that at that time. This was way before the civil rights movement of the 60's. Those guys just gave me hell for letting a colored person sit down. I told them, *"If you want these people to go to the back of the bus and there isn't any back left, what do you expect them to do?"* I am proud that I did that even if I did catch hell.

Bivouac

During our last training sessions the pilots were given training on flying tight formations and the ground crew went on bivouac at Myrtle Beach, South Carolina. This is where the cooks were trained to feed men on small rations and we were trained on how to survive in the jungle or whatever obstacles should come our way.

Still waiting for my papers to show up, we went back to the airfield and got ready to go overseas. There was a particular day that I will not forget. I had been selected to FLY overseas instead of going on a boat like the rest of the ground crew. What a deal. I wanted to fly so bad. I was shocked. I'll never know why I was singled out and given this privilege.

Back Row: Bernero, Rudy, Hughes, Mullens
Front Row: Aydelotte, Good, Nordstrom, Hysa, Childress, Herring, and "Queenie"

I was hooked up with Pilot Lt. Bill Hughes from Texas and Co-Pilot Lt. Norbit Rudy of Wisconsin. The other members were Lt. Johnny Benero as Bombardier and Lt. William Mullens as Navigator. The enlisted men were, Paul Hysa, and his dog Queenie, Johnny Nordstrom, Lloyd Childress, Marion Collier, Don Aydelotte, Hershel Good and myself. I was a corporal until I arrived overseas and then I was made a Sergeant.

NEW YORK

We took off in a B24 trainer plane and headed for New York to get our new airplane and head overseas. I had never been in an airplane until this day. I was finally going to get to fly. Little did I know how well I would get to know the inside of an airplane. We had a few days to spend in New York and got to go to town every evening. We saw the musician, Fred Waring and The Pennsylvanians, Time Square, Rockefeller Center and The Rockettes, a play (Life With Father), and the Ice Capades. I had never been to a big city like New York. We had a good time.

We finally got our new B24 bomber airplane and departed for Florida, the first stop of our long journey. We spent one day in Florida and after receiving more fuel, we took off for British Guinea for our next fueling.

BELEM, BRAZIL

Then we were on to Belem, Brazil. We landed in Belem in early afternoon. Some of us decided we would walk into the jungle which was right on the edge of the runway. None of us had ever seen a jungle before. The closest I ever came to seeing a real jungle was when I read my first book, <u>Bamba the Jungle Boy of Jaguar Island</u>. We hadn't walked into that jungle 10 feet until we were in a thick tangled up undergrowth. It turned out that it wasn't a smart thing for us to do as we got into ants! Mosquitos swarmed us and there was every kind of big bug you could think of on my face! A little different than the woods I hunted at home. We got the heck out of there and back to the barracks they had built in the clearing.

Jungle in Belem, Brazil

SHORT SNORTER CLUB

I became a member of the Short Snorter Club. A Short Snorter is a banknote inscribed by people traveling together on an aircraft. The tradition was started by Alaskan Bush flyers in the 1920s and spread through the military and commercial aviation. During World War II short snorters were signed by flight crews and conveyed good luck to soldiers crossing the Atlantic. Friends would take the local currency and sign each others bills creating a "keepsake of your buddy's signatures".

Brazil was warm and tropical. Another new experience for me.

NATAL, BRAZIL

The next day we were off to Natal, Brazil where we spent the next eleven days. We had such a long wait because there were so many planes waiting to leave. We landed at Natal too late for Christmas dinner in 1943, so the Mess Sergeant told us we could have some pineapples to hold us over until the evening meal. Little did we know we were going to have to live on pineapples for the next eleven days. It seemed that the ship bringing the food had been sunk, so there was no meat for anyone for awhile. During that eleven days that we were in Brazil we got to just lounge around, play games or go to town. We were near a beach so we spent some time there as well. I had never seen a beach before.

The Pied Piper Nose Art

While we were waiting to go overseas there was a native artist painter that was painting decals of all kinds on the planes. One of the enlisted men asked Lt. Bill Hughes if we could have a lady painted on the nose of our plane. He sure didn't care so this is where the nose art, "The Pied Piper", was painted on the fuselage of our plane. WE LOVED IT! The only trouble was that when we finally got to Italy the CO instructed us hire one of the local artists to paint pants on the naked lady. We weren't the only ones. All the crews who had nudity in their nose art were instructed to have them re-painted. After seeing pictures of "The Pied Piper", I don't believe we ever got that re-painting done.

While in town I bought a pair of silk stockings and sent them home to my wife, Bette. Such things were not easy to find in the US. One shop had some leather engineer boots for sale for $5.00 so we all bought a pair.

"The Pied Piper"

Finally, it was our turn and we were awakened at 4:00am to leave. They had filled our Tokyo reserve tanks so full of gas for the long trip that when we leveled off the gas overflowed off the top of the wing and was only missing the fire from our superchargers by a couple feet! The gas could have easily run into the fire. This was our first big scare of the war.

The radio operator called the tower and ask for permission to land. But, they said *"just fly around for awhile and transfer the extra fuel."*

We had known about a plane blowing up a couple days sooner and it dawned on us that this could have been the reason. Thankfully this didn't happen to us and we finally continued on to Dakar, Africa.

DAKAR, AFRICA

Lt. Mullins must have been good at his job as we hit Dakar right on time. They were keeping the string of B24's moving along so we didn't spend much time there and were sent on to Merrakech the next day.

B24s

MERRAKECH, AFRICA

We landed in Merrakech and were told that the locals would kill any dogs they found so we decided to sleep all night in the airplane to keep our cocker spaniel, Queenie safe. She was our mascot and we meant to protect her.

There was a big scary looking native sentry guarding our airplanes walking the beat with a bayonet as sharp as a pinpoint over his shoulder. He stopped at our airplane and wanted Collier's boots. Collier would not give up his new boots even with us telling him he should just give them to him to get him out of there. The guard had a leather pouch about 2 inches square around his arm. I really wanted to have it and I tried to bargain with him. He couldn't be without it as it kept the evil spirits away. He told me that he would go get another one. That way he would always have one with him, and he would trade me for it when he got back. We took off before he returned. That sure would have been a good thing to have brought home.

Merrakech was an English owned field and was only allowed so many planes. We got orders to leave for our next base even though there was a storm between there and Tunis, Africa which is where we were going. They cleared us at 13,000 feet. The mountains were higher than that so Lt. Bill Hughes decided maybe we could go above the storm. When we hit that storm all hell broke loose. We lost 5000 feet in 30 seconds! We were falling out of the sky like a rock. Co-Pilot Rudy put his chute on and rang the first bell to jump. Bill the pilot said, *"ok."* He meant, ok, you can take over the plane, but Rudy thought he meant "ok" ring the second bell to jump. The second bell meant "go." Aydelotte and I had our chutes on and the escape door open. The wind was thrashing through the plane. It was hard to stand up. Collier was trying to get us to jump. We didn't know what to do. I sure didn't want to jump. All we could see below were mountains! Collier was not going to be able to jump as his chute was laying in the tail turret and he couldn't get to it. Man, his eyes were bigger than silver dollars. The plane was rocking and rolling so bad you couldn't move. We didn't want to leave Collier. We just stood there hanging on and not wanting to jump. The pilot finally got the plane leveled out. We were glad we stuck it out. This was our second big scare in the war with many more to come. I guess it wasn't my time.

ALGIERS, AFRICA

When Algiers came into view they decided to land and check out the airplane. It had taken quite a beating during that ordeal in the storm. Lt. Mullins had a 5th of whiskey which didn't last long after the ground got kissed many times. Collier swore the wing bent straight backward. The mechanics removed the cowling to check out the wing structure to assure it was in good enough condition to fly.

Inside the B24

TUNIS, AFRICA

The plane was ok, so the next day we went on to Tunis, our original destination. This is where we had to stay for about 10 days until the CB's (construction battalion) got our landing strips built in Italy. This was an extremely boring 10 days. The only thing we were able to do was go to see movies that were shown on a screen in a hanger. There wasn't room for everyone to sit down. The soldiers that were stationed there didn't like us taking all of the chairs that were there and complained. After this complaint, the Master Sergeant stopped us at the door and said to Lt. Mullens, *"Hey, Bud, you can't go in there yet."* Lt. Mullens replied, *"It's Lieutenant to you."* This embarrassed the Master Sergeant and he apologized and proceeded to explain why we had to wait. Lt. Mullens understood and jumped up on a barrel and said, *"Alright you flying bastards, we can't go in until 7:30, but who the hell wants to wait until 7:30!"* He then jumped down off the barrel and we waited until 7:30. The Master Sergeant hadn't known he was outranked because all we had on were coveralls.

B-24 Liberators flying over the Adriatic to bomb targets in Northern Italy.

SAN GIOVANNI, ITALY

The front lines were only a little ways up the boot in Italy when we landed. We could actually hear the artillery; the big guns. At the new landing strips the CB's had put steel mats at the end of the new runways and we had never landed on anything like that before. They were 8 ft. long and 3 ft. wide mesh steel that were connected together and placed over gravel. When our wheels hit those steel mats it made a terrifying noise. It was like fire crackers going off under the plane! It scared us to death. This was the 3rd scare of the war with many more to come. We had finally reached what would be our home base in San Giovanni, Italy near Cerignola. This is the base that we would fly in and out of for the duration of the war. It was our home away from home.

Laying Metal Mats on Newly Cleared Runway

When the CB's cleared the area to build our runways they saved what buildings they could so we could use them as orderly room headquarters. We had a barn that was converted to a mess hall. There was a stucco building that was our headquarters. We had no hangers in which to repair airplanes. All repairs had to be done on the planes outside. The weather was not always good and that meant the mechanics would have to change a motor out in the open. I sure gave them a lot of credit for working in those conditions. I knew it wasn't easy.

Overhauling Done Out in the Open

I was now a Staff Sergeant and a member of the 739 Bomb Squadron of the 454th Bomb Group of the 15th Air Force.

There were a lot of our airbases within about 50 miles of Foggia, Italy. The San Giovanni base was really very primitive. I am sure they all were. You would have thought that with so many men in a close proximity, there could have been wells dug so we could have running water. No such luck. For a bathroom we had a large pit, dug by the Italian locals, with an enclosure around it. There was a 2 x 4 board to sit on. It was pretty crude, but it worked. When the pit got full or a bit rank, we would have them fill it in and dig another one.

Church Across From USO

It was only 6 or 7 miles into Cerignola where there was a pretty big USO (United Service Organization). This is a private, nonprofit organization that provides morale and recreational services to members of the armed forces. It was right down town across from a big church with a dome that looked like the capital building. At the USO there were pool tables and other entertainment. Soldiers from many of the air bases went to this USO. It wasn't hard to catch a GI truck going that way. There was also a barber there and we could get our haircut for 20 lire.

That would be about twenty cents in American money. There was usually a softball game going on that you could get into at anytime. There was an English group that had some anti-aircraft guns set up around the bases. I never saw these anti-aircraft guns ever used. About the only time that we would see these English guys was at the USO when there was a soccer game with a group from another field. It was a blast just listening to those bloody blips. Ha Ha.

When we would get back to San Giovanni from a bombing mission, the Red Cross girl was always there with donuts and drink. It was always the same girl. I would say she was in her late 20's. She was not a beauty queen but any girls looked good after being away so long. She was very pleasant. She had to take a lot from all the GIs. Those donuts carried me for a long time as I would be too late for dinner and the oxygen had made me so tired that I would sleep right through the supper hour. Then the next morning I would wake up with ten minutes until briefing for the next mission. There just wasn't much time to eat.

There were two runways at this field, one for us and one parallel to ours for the 455th group. This close proximity proved to be a problem. When we took off, our prop wash, which is the wind off the props, went over the end of their runway and theirs over ours. This caused a terrible down draft for B24's when they took off loaded with 6000lbs. of bombs.

It was February and the weather was also a problem when we started flying missions. Wing headquarters told us, the 454th Bomb Group, that they would like 8 photographers on every mission. We didn't even have an aerial photographer on our roster so four of us from the photo division volunteered to fly and take pictures of the bomb spots. Ross, Hawks, Wilson, and of course myself. We hadn't even seen a K24 aerial camera before that time, but we soon learned that there wasn't much to it. You just plugged them into the 24 volt system and turned them on and all you had to do is point them to the ground where the bombs were landing.

We photographers were allowed to go to the pilot's briefings. The gunners had their own briefing. The gunners weren't even told what the target was, just how many fighters to expect. We photographers were pretty popular with the gunners as they could ask us where we were going and how many heavy guns would be shooting at us. Eventually some of the pilots became a bit leery of us because most of the first planes that got shot down seemed to have a photographer on board.

Briefing

I guess the Generals thought we needed some breaking in so they sent us on three what we called "milk runs" to targets in Northern Italy. A milk run was a easy job with little or no danger.

The orders for so many photographers on each mission bothered us so we sent out word that we would like to have volunteers from cooks, armors, mechanics, medics, or clerical help to fly missions to take pictures of the bomb spots. These so called "milk runs" seemed to help us recruit for the job because the rule was if you flew 50 missions you could go home. These volunteers thought they could fly 50 easy milk run missions and go home. Piece of cake. So they thought.

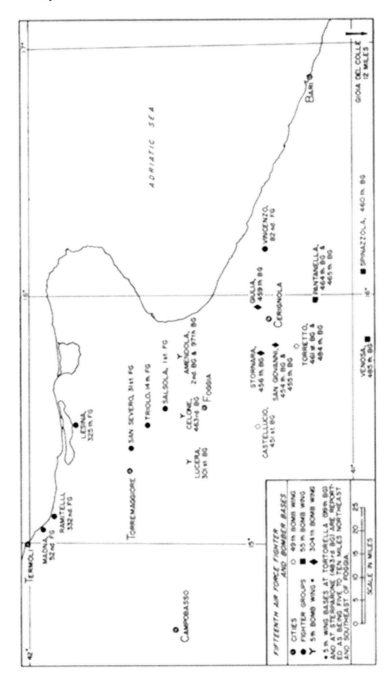

Map of Air Bases in Italy

FLAK

B24's Flying through Flak

ORVIETA AIRFIELD

Our first mission on February 8, 1944 was the Orvieta Airfield in northern Italy. The Germans had began to use this airfield to fight the incoming bombers, mainly us. I remember at the pilot's briefing they stressed to the pilots that they had to keep a tight formation or the enemy fighters would get them. There weren't many fighters or much flak at this first mission and all planes returned unharmed. This didn't seem to bad. Flak was flying pieces of metal from the shells fired at us from the ground timed to explode at a certain altitude.

The second mission was a railroad marshaling yard in northern Italy that wasn't very well protected either. A marshalling yard is a railway yard in which trains are assembled and goods are loaded. Again, all planes returned to base.

The plane mechanics would watch for their special plane to return. That was their pride and joy as they were responsible for that certain plane.

The weather was so unpredictable in late February and early March that we would only get to fly about a third of the time.

When we finally got to go on the third mission it was the docks at Trieste, Italy, which I presume the Germans were using to re-supply their troops in Italy. Again, no losses.

Mt. Vesuvius

B24's Flying Too Close to Eruption of Mt. Vesuvius

Another obstacle was the eruption of the volcano, Mt. Vesuvius. It caused major problems for the newly-arrived allied forces in Italy when ash and rocks from the eruption destroyed planes and forced evacuations at nearby airbases. The heat melted paint from planes many were scorched.

YUGOSLAVIA

In mid March we really got into the thick of it. On this forth mission we would have been ok, but again those briefings had scared our pilots so badly by telling them that if they fell out of formation they were duck soup for the German fighters. We headed across the Adriatic Sea to hit the Cecina Railroad Bridge, a target in Yugoslavia. When we reached land we would be flying at 20,000 feet. The plans were that after we dropped our bombs we would swing around back over of the Adriatic Sea and drop back down to 13,000 feet for the return trip home. One of our planes in the position that we called high right lost his superchargers and couldn't keep the altitude and began falling out of formation. Just what they were warned about in briefing. We had started or final approach to drop bombs. Because the pilot being briefed on fighters so thoroughly he decided he would start his turn to go back over the Adriatic and fall in with us when we dropped down to an altitude he could maintain. The big problem was, I guess he didn't realize we were starting to drop bombs as he swung under us. As we were on the approach I was watching out of the escape hatch where my camera was mounted. I saw him sliding across under us and I yelled out loud, '*get out of there!*" I froze my cheeks watching as the third bomb in the string struck him on the right wing. This caused a huge explosion under us that made our plane jolt up! Then there was a call from the pilot to ask what that flak had done to us. Real quickly I answered, "*THAT WASNT FLAK, WE JUST DROPPED BOMBS ON ONE OF OUR OWN B24's!*" Our bombardier just went crazy. I remember telling him, "*this is war and he did as he was trained to do just as you were doing as you were trained to do.*" Our pilot that we hit had made a fatal mistake. The rest of us returned unharmed but this was our first loss and there was much sadness in the whole group that evening. That got be a normal thing and had to be soon forgotten.

The ideal amount of planes to send on each mission was 42. Because of losses we seldom had that many.

ANZIO, ITALY

It was slow going for the allied forces all the way up the boot of Italy. This was mostly because of all of the religious monasteries located there. These religious and historic locations were off limits. The Germans knew this and they would take advantage of the situation by using these monasteries as places to set up their heavy guns. The allies could not touch them. There was a monastery called Monte Cassino along the western coast of Italy just outside of Rome. For many months our ground troops tried to make their way up through this area but couldn't go any further because of this disadvantage. The US military dignitaries struggled with the decisions to destroy this fortress. They could see the Germans entering and leaving this location from the air. On February 15, 1944 the order was given to bomb this facility. This was a huge detriment to the Germans, but they returned. In March my bombardment group was ordered to bomb it again. We were high altitude bombers and had difficulty bombing down low. We managed to get the job done. There wasn't much left. Moving ahead for a bit to when I was in the hospital. There was a conversation about this mission to bomb the monastery. There was an English boy in the hospital as well. I remember that he was teased a lot and I gave him credit because he took it all very well. He would say, *"the English is the bloody best fighters."* Of course he got a counter phrase thrown at him as one boy spoke up, *"the only time you see an Englishman was at the retreat of Dunkirk and in a rest camp!"* He came back with, *"when the German planes come the allies run. When the English planes come over the Germans run. When the Americans come over, EVERYBODY RUNS!"* He said this because of the raid at the Monte Cassino Monastery. He said that because the Germans knew we were coming and fled the monastery and after it was all over they returned. He was a great kid and I enjoyed him.

Monte Cassino Before and After Bombing

Remains of Monte Cassino

Monte Cassino destruction of the monestary

P38 Fighter Plane Escorted B24 Bombers

FRANKFURT, GERMANY

I guess the powers that be thought we were ready for the big time as the next mission was to be to Frankfort, Germany. This was a lot further out than we had ever gone and of course more fighters and more flak than we had ever seen before. This mission opened a lot of eyes as what would lie ahead of us. This was to be a pretty long mission. We were awakened at around 5am and told briefing would be in 30 minutes.

That is how I learned to drink very hot coffee as we had to drink it out of a big urn of maybe 50 gallon and was it ever hot! We didn't have time to eat much. The cooks would make us some pancakes but all we had to put on them was orange marmalade. I would get a couple bites and head for briefing. Briefing was a very long meeting compared to the first two or three because we had to be aware of so many more things, such as estimated amount of heavy guns shooting from the ground and how many fighter planes we expected to encounter. We did expect our P38's to help us out but their range wasn't nearly far enough to help us return to base. P38's were the fighter planes that would escort the bombers. Intelligence was right. Just as they had said, there were many fighters and a lot of flak to protect the target. Flak was intense. The sky was full of this flying metal. We lost three planes that day. This got us into the heat of war real quick. In one of those planes was my buddy, Ross. We had chummed with him and his wife in Charleston. I never saw his plane go down, but I did see the one on our right. I saw three chutes get out of this one and I hoped more that I didn't see. This was our first photographer loss so the photo lab was quiet that evening. I had never lost a friend before. Ross and I had become best of friends and now my heart just broke, but I had to learn to place these feelings somewhere other than my heart.

Me and My Buddy Ross

Col. Gun Presenting Me with Air Medal

After about 16 missions Colonel Gun awarded me with the air medal for meritorious achievement in aerial flight while participating in sustained operational activities against the enemy. This was an award that was attained after flying 5 combat missions. Each 5 missions after that you would receive an oak leaf cluster to put on the ribbon. I was very proud.

K24 Aircraft Camera

BUCHAREST, ROMANIA

We were just beginning to train the volunteers to run the camera, but hadn't sent any up on a mission yet. The very next mission was to the Bucharest rail marshaling yards. We lost Wilson, another photographer on this mission. We were told by some guys in his squadron that they thought most of the men had gotten out but that is all they knew. We did get word a couple weeks later that he had been picked up and was a prisoner of war in Germany. Now we are down to just two of the four of us that started flying these missions. Very quickly we started getting our volunteers into rotation. Either myself or Sgt. Hawks would have to go along to insure that we would get pictures.

I had flown the first 16 missions and with the poor eating habits and the tension I developed a bad case of yellow jaundice. I had become very weak and was turning yellow. We had a crude infirmary that I went to where they decided that I needed to go to the hospital. There they could bring me out of it with a strict diet. I went to the hospital in Bari, Italy. I was finally getting some rest. I remember that they would press on my side where my liver was and make me cough. The medics could feel how enlarged the liver was. Lt. Graves came to see me and brought me a chocolate candy bar that I hid under my pillow. When no one was looking I would take a bite. Chocolate was not allowed on my diet. I was on this diet for seven days. As I recovered my diet was returned to regular meals. I was on a regular diet for two days before they sent me back to the base. The cook there would make meatballs out of c-rations, which was some kind of canned meat. They were really pretty good. There was another kid there named Peters with the same problem. He was still on a very strick diet when I told him how good those meatballs were. He asked me for some so I gave them to him. The nurse happened to see me give them to him and yelled at him, *"what did you do with those meatballs!"* Peters had crammed them in his mouth really quick so she couldn't take it away from him.

There was a fellow running around the hospital that was as orange as a pumpkin. The next day after Peters and I saw this guy the doctor asked Me and three other patients that were almost well to carry him on a stretcher out to the ambulance. I asked the doctor what had happened. He told me and these other guys to sit down that he wanted to have a little talk with us. He said, *"that guy has been here three times with jaundice and he is in really bad shape. He could possibly die. That's how bad he is, so I am sending him back to the United States. And, if you guys ever get this again you do exactly as you are told. It is very serious.*" He made believers out of us.

Hawks and the volunteers took care of things while I was gone. We did happen to lose two of the other photographers before I returned to duty. The very next mission the plane Hawks was flying in got a direct hit over the target from flak which eliminated that crew and another photographer. I think that is why some pilots became a little afraid of hauling photographers because it seemed that those were the planes most often shot down. This left me as the only photographer that started these missions. The odds were not in my favor.

Some of the volunteers did ok but some did not. I took over the task of assigning these guys each day. I knew which of these volunteers I could depend on. One particular day when I didn't go I met them as they returned and one of the volunteers said, "*I didn't get any pictures. I didn't even get back with the camera.*" He said that as he was getting ready to set his K24 camera in the rack, the rack blew up and he either had to drop the camera or fall out! So he dropped the camera. I was familiar with the situation as the hatches were real light and would blow up with the wind as it came up through the hatch. All I could say is, "*the Germans will think we are running out of bombs and are now dropping cameras on them.*"

VIENNA, AUSTRIA

The next mission was a long and tough one to Vienna, Austria. We were estimating 327 heavy guns would be shooting at us, as well as all the expected fighters. Again, our P38 fighter cover was great going up to the target, but there was no help coming back.

Don Aydelotte Our Gunner

We were in trouble. We were smothered by all the planes the Germans had; ME109's, JU88's and FW190's. They all got into the act. We shot some of them down but that usually meant we lost some bombers as well. This fighting in the air was so scary. We could tell when a young inexperienced German pilot was in the plane as they would just dive right into our formation with little caution to our 50 caliber guns located in every plane. He might get a bomber but our gunners would get him. The more experienced pilots would stay further out and send their 20 millimeter shells at us and peal off for another run. If the sun was shining they would also take advantage of it by flying between us and the sun so we wouldn't be able to spot them so easily.

The next day after this mission I was going to take the day off and send some of my best volunteers up to cover the bomb spots. I couldn't believe what happened about 8am. While I was still resting in my bunk, I had someone awaken me and said, "Hey White, *you ARE here!*" It was the 1st Sergeant who had been talking to Pate, a friend of mine who was another occupant of our tent. He had told Pate, "*it is too bad we lost White yesterday on 941.*" Of course Pate told him that I was in our tent and in the sack. He was just checking it out to see if it was really me. He said to me, "*I have already sent in the morning report with you missing in action. Would you mind going over to the base headquarters and see if you can get your name taken off the list?*" I definitely didn't want my name on that list as that would mean a telegram would be sent to Bette of my missing status. When I got to the intelligence office I found an older gentleman named Captain Burge. He told me that the list had already gone back to wing headquarters at Bari, Italy, but he would get on the cranker telephone and see if he could get my name removed. He was finally successful. That took a load off my mind. I was glad I switched planes the morning before, as I was originally flying on 941. I had changed planes to get a better place in the formation. All of this would not have been true if I hadn't changed planes. Guess it wasn't my time.

STEYR, AUSTRIA

On April 2nd we boarded the plane for a mission to Steyr, Austria to hit the airplane factory there. They were one of the biggest providers of the German fighters. We just had to do something to eliminate some of these fighters. This turned out to be one of toughest missions. Flak and fighters were on us. It was a frantic situation. Another huge battle in the sky. We lost a couple more planes before returning to San Giovanni air strip.

Bombing Ploesti

PLOESTI, ROMANIA

The next mission would be to Ploesti, the big Romanian oil fields. Our boys had hit that field coming from Africa a few months earlier. This previous mission was almost a disaster as it was just too far for the amount of gas our planes could hold.

During this previous mission they had decided to go in at low altitude, trying to create a surprise, but not thinking about the fire that would come from those big tanks blowing up. They were so low that it scorched the paint off some of the planes. They did cause a lot of damage, but the Germans had got everything back in operation before this day's mission. This was to be a very long mission with a lot of fighters to intercept us on the way. Believe it or not we had a full flight plan with the complete formation of 42 airplanes ready to go. Most generally we couldn't get that many ready as some would be disabled and would need new engines or sometime the fuselage repaired or various other repairs. The intelligence was right on because when we flew near Romania we went right over the Karlova airfield in Bulgaria, which housed most of the ME109 German fighter planes in that area. Of course they came flying up to stop our progress. We had some P38 fighter planes flying along with us that helped but a lot of them were right on us. What an air battle took place! We lost some P38's and the Germans lost some ME109's. We only lost one of our B24's during that struggle, but the Germans had decided they needed to protect their oil supply so they had set up almost 300 anti-aircraft heavy guns for protection.

We received another surprise.

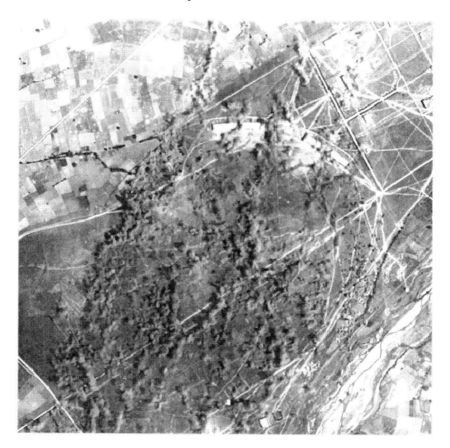

Bombing Karlova, Bulgaria

Our P38's saw some other planes coming. It was our new P51's fighters to help us across the target and part way back home! We all thanked God that help had arrived. These new P51's were the Cadillac of fighters. Our gunners had not been told of these new fighter escorts. There had been rumors of the German fighters dropping aerial bombs through the formation, so when one of our gunners saw the P51's drop their wing tanks he thought it was the Germans and shot some rounds at the P51! Luckily he missed. This mission took it's toll on our bombers as we lost 3 more during this bomb run.

Willow Run, Michigan B24 Factory.

The United States knew we would need a lot of replacement airplanes as well as more men. We would lose a crew out of the tent next to us and a new crew would move in. Sometimes you wouldn't even get to know this new crew until they would get shot down and another new crew would move in.

P51 Fighter Plane

New B24's were built at a rate of 1 per hour at Willow Run, Michigan. We would lose them just as fast as they were built. The next morning in front of the headquarter building was a P51 with a sign saying **DONT SHOOT THIS!** Everyone knew what had happened, but were sure glad to have this much needed help on the bomb runs.

I feel that the presence of the P51's was the big turning point in the war. The cost of men and the cost of making all of the bombing raids was tremendous. The P51's that came to our defense were flown by the Tuskegee Airmen. These African-American pilots were truly lifesavers. Black fighter pilots fought with us and proved that they could shoot down enemy aircraft as well as their white counterparts.

When we got replacement crews, they would be split up and each of the members placed with a seasoned crew. One day we were given a young man to fly in the ball turret. He was really young and not very big. You couldn't get into the turret if you were very big. One day we had a very rough mission and everyone was firing their 50 caliber guns from their turrets except him. Someone called to him and asked him why he wasn't shooting at the German planes. He sounded like he was crying as he said that he couldn't see. It turned out that someone in the front used the relief tube and the urine had sprayed all over his windows. Also, he had wet his pants and the 24 volt heated suit that he was wearing was shocking him. I know that young lad must have lost 20 years growth in those 15 minutes.

When we started flying missions, we just had fleece lined suits. This was a pair of pants and a coat. They were not very warm but they were better than nothing because it was so very cold at those high altitudes. The warmest I remember it being at 20,000 feet was 19 degrees below zero centigrade. Soon we got electric heated suits that looked like the old time long underwear. They were blue with a lot of electric wires in them. All we had to do was plug them in to the 24 volt system and they warmed up pretty good. I would look like a round ball with a hat that came down over my ears. We would wear overalls over the electric suit. We had boots that were kind of like the ones I used to wear hunting. We were issued flak vests to wear but none of us like to wear them. The reason I didn't was because I always wore a backpack parachute and the flak vest would not fit around me. We would lay our flak vests on the floor and stand on them. I doubt if that would have helped much if we had received a direct hit. I preferred to wear my chute.

MUNICH, GERMANY

Munich had a big airport that was essential to the German supply train so we had this target in our sights next. There were a lot of heavy guns there also and we didn't do so good again as far as losses.

We must have lost two more planes this day. It was getting to be a normal day for us.

So many mornings we would line up to get on the run way for take off and the flares would appear to tell us the mission is canceled because of bad weather over the target. This happened a lot at the start of our missions back in March and April. Later on we would be given an alternate target or we might drop on what we called "ETA" or estimated time of arrival. This is dropping bombs based on calculations of time over target. This was somewhat successful, but of course, not as good as direct sight. We had lost 4 of the volunteer photographers, and I was wondering when it would be my turn. It was always on my mind. I always wore a backpack parachute. I had seen too many men get thrown or sucked out of an airplane without a chute. If this happened to me at least I would have a fighting chance.

Bombing Budapest

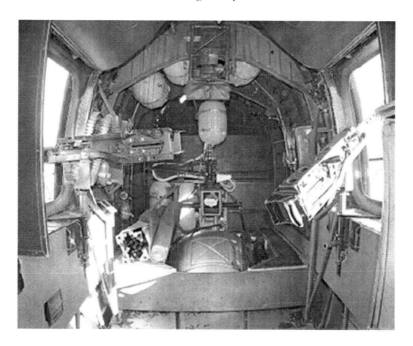

Waste Gunner Position

When we dropped through the clouds on an ETA bombing run, the photographers might as well have stayed home. In this case there was a reconnaissance plane that went and took pictures of the damage. Sometimes the bombardiers were told just to drop on the lead planes bombs away order so all they had to do is salvo the bombs as they heard the order.

Volunteer Photographer

BUDAPEST, HUNGARY

The next mission was to the Budapest main marshaling yard. The group bombardier, who was a Major, and of course what I called a "big shot", was to be the lead man and everyone would drop on his command. I happened to be taking pictures and I could see that we had done a very poor job. At interrogation I told the intelligence officer just that, that we done a very poor job, and that we got a few bombs in the yards but most of them went up the hillside. Boy, was that hot shot Major mad! My answer to him was to wait until the pictures come in and we will see.

Of course when he saw the pictures he said that I had taken pictures of someone else's bombs. I said, *"just how could I."* Just because he was a big shot he thought he couldn't have been that wrong. We always wanted to do a good job but I think a lot of guys were tickled to see this "big shot" be wrong. He was so big on himself. Two more of our B24's didn't make it back although one of them ditched in the Adriatic Sea so I expect they might have been picked up out of the drink.

Bombing Budapest

SOFIA TOWN, BULGARIA

The next day, on Sunday morning, the mission was to Sofia Town, Bulgaria with 20lb frag bombs; 240 in each bomb bay. You multiply this by 40 airplanes and that makes the sky just full of these little devils. We were told at briefing that the Germans made the Romanians work in their factories. Some of them would get away when we bombed and we thought it would help the war effort to help them get away.

Queenie

This day I lucked out when I found out that Bill Hughes was flying in the formation where I could get some good pictures. It didn't happen very often but I was glad when I got to fly with the men I flew over with. I met my old crew at briefing and they told me that Queenie was in heat! They said they had fastened her in the tent while they were gone. I just laughed at them for thinking that the tent would keep all the Italian local dogs from getting to her. Sure enough, when we got back I walked to their tent with them and there were about a dozen dogs that had her out of the tent and were breeding her. When I came back by their tent, they had decided to give Queenie a douche! This was probably the funniest thing I saw the whole time I was gone. Someone came along and told them the last dog to breed her was going to be the daddy of the pups.

Hughes, Childres, Mullens, Good, Bernero & Queenie

They knew of another Cocker Spaniel in the next bomb group and they took her over to have this dog breed her. I do know that Childres took her home after they completed their missions and she had pups. I don't know if any of them spoke English. Ha Ha

I was the only photographer left from the original crew, so I was given the task of placing volunteer photographers in the planes I thought would be the best for pictures. One of the volunteers had flown six missions and was getting really scared. He came to me and said, *"Wayne, I am scared."* *"Yes,"* I told him, *"I am too. Everyone is scared."* *I am afraid I won't get back,"* he said. And with this I told him, *"don't go then."* I told him he could go back to putting bombs in the bays just like he was doing before. He thought the other guys would call him yellow. I told him, *"not the ones that have been up there they won't."* But, he insisted he would go tomorrow. So, I told him I would put him in a new airplane that we had just gotten in that had a camera hatch. That suited him ok. I guess he must have had a premonition. The next morning that plane never got into the air. It exploded on the runway. I think it was because of the prop wash from the other runway. A situation I spoke of earlier. I just remember him as a short punchy round faced kid. I don't even remember his name or where he was from. Damn this war.

There was one thing good about being overseas. No one had to do KP duty. We hired the local Italians to perform this task. Some guys had Italians come to their tents and get their clothes and wash them along with other duties.

Lt. Graves asked me to slow down on the amount of missions I was flying as he needed me and didn't want to lose me. It would have caused him a lot more work. Of course he wanted me to fly 4 hours a month and get my flight pay but he also realized that all of our dreams was to finish our missions and go home. Even though none of us had achieved 50 missions yet there was still a light at the end of the tunnel.

One day I was flying a training mission with Bill Hughes. Lt. Weir was flying on our right wing. I was in the waste wing with a K20 camera taking his picture. He saw me taking his picture and decided to get just as close as he could. In fact, he moved in so close that I could stepped out of the window onto his wing! His prop wasn't far from the back of our right wing. *"WHAT THE HECK IS HE DOING!"* I yelled. Then I realized that as long as he could see me there taking pictures he was not going to quit so I moved out of the window and out of sight. Whew!

Lt. Weir on Our Right Side

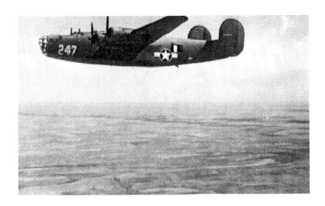

Lt. Weir Flying Too Close

When we landed Bill Hughes just read Lt. Weir the riot act! He told him, *"Don't you EVER do that again!"* Lt. Weir thought of me as his buddy because I would take his film from his camera and develop it for him when I wasn't busy. I also would take film from the end of a used roll from my big K24 camera and cut it into strips and paste it into his 120 film cartridge so he could take more pictures. He was definitely a camera bug.

One of our biggest contests among the crews is to see which one could build the best stove. We cut a 55 gallon drum in half with a machete. Then we went to the bone yard of the wrecked B24's and got some gas lines. We would have the chief braze the gas line in a fuel drum that we would put outside the tent and put the line underground up into the tent and under the drum. You could make a blow torch and have a coil of line in the barrel to make the gas into vapor. This would make a white hot fire. It wasn't anything to see a tent on fire at the flap on top because the chimney would get so hot.

My Tent in San Giovanni

The Hotel Pied Piper

When you go to pilot training you all go together until the flight instructor decides if you would be better in a bomber or a fighter. They all got to know each other in their first courses and remained friends. On one particular day one of the P38 pilots came flying over our field and he knew which tent his buddy from the first training was in so he came in low and just as he got to the bomber pilots tents he set it straight up and rolling. This prop wash tore the tent down. This was just a prank, but it sure was funny.

VIENNA, AUSTRIA

The enemy had radar that could tell them our altitude. They could set the flak to burst at this altitude which caused us so much trouble and so many losses. We were inserting something new to help fowl up the enemy radar. We were given large boxes of chaff to throw out the window when we got near the target. This chaff was just exactly like Christmas tree tinsel. These tinfoil pieces would fill the air and cause their radar fits as to just how high we were. We used these pieces of tinfoil for the rest of our missions and it was somewhat successful. I say somewhat because we did however, lose three planes on this day. One to flak and two to enemy fighters. I will always remember this Vienna mission as they had the most anti-aircraft guns as any target we hit.

I guess all is fair in war. With us finding out things that would foul them up, they were also finding things to disrupt our bombardment of their much needed factories and oil supply. The last trip to the Ploesti oil fields found us with another obstacle. They had built smoke screens so that when they got the word that we were coming they would light the smoke screens so that the targets would not be visible to our bombardiers. Guess turnabout is fair play.

We made 20 raids to the Ploesti oil fields to cut off the Germans oil supply. These were pretty rough trips for many reasons. We were told at briefing that if we got shot down we should try to get to a German soldier and turn ourselves in because the local citizens would pitchfork us if they got to us first. The targets were heavily fortified with heavy guns and they had learned to put up smoke screens so we couldn't see the targets. In addition to this problem there was the Karlova airfield which housed most of the ME109's German fighters in this area.

B24 Hit By Flak

KARLOVA, BULGARIA

One day we played a dirty trick on them. We filled our bombay full of 20lb frag bombs. Each plane would carry 240 of these little frag bombs which broke on contact sending fragments in every direction. Our intelligence people had figured just how long they could fly without refueling so we flew just far enough out to give them time to land at the airbase to refuel. Then we did a 180 degree turn and came back over the airfield as they were refueling and dropped our bombs on them on the ground. This was quite a success as we were credited with destroying 75% of their fighters in one day! We did, however, lose a couple of B24's that day. I believed we had dealt a serious blow to the German Luftwaffe. This is what they called the German Air Force.

Stars & Stripes Newspaper

About once a week I would receive mail from home. I would get letters from my Mother, Sister, and Bette almost every day. It took about two weeks for a letter to arrive. My Mother would send cookies that were usually all crumbled by the time they got there. They were great though. We all got to read the Stars & Stripes government paper that helped keep us informed of how the war was progressing. I received my hometown newspaper the Macomb Journal.

One day I was looking over the Journal and all at once I felt someone tap me on my shoulder and low and behold, who could it be, but Marne Selby from my hometown, Colchester, Illinois. We had hunted and fished together most of our teenage years. Probably one of my best friends during those years. There we were together in Italy. He was a gunner for the 456th bomb group just across the runway from us. Someone had told him in a letter from home that I was stationed there near him so he just decided to walk over to our place and see if he could find me. Since I was looking at the Macomb paper that I received from home, he decided to look at the section of the paper that told where the local servicemen were scattered over the globe. The first name he came to was Jerry Lee Hulson. With this he tore that paper up and grabbed another one. Sure enough there was Jerry Lee Hulson's name again. He tore that paper up also. Jerry was in Marne's class in school and they were not the best of friends. It seemed that Jerry's name was in nearly every paper. He was from an upper crust family and Marne was not so that was probably most of the problem. It just happened to be payday and of course that meant a big crap game that night. Marne was just like his dad, Clem, who really liked to gamble. Marne decided to stay and get into the game that night. I guess they didn't have a game like that on his base. He didn't do very well in the crap game and he couldn't wait until next month. We discussed what had happened on the missions he had flown and what we expected from here on. He had to get back as he didn't know if his crew would be scheduled to fly the next day. That was the last time I saw him as he got shot down the very next week. The only way I knew this was because it was in the Macomb paper that he was missing. He did parachute out and was a POW for the rest of the war. I never saw him again until after the war was over and he was back in Colchester.

Me and Marne Selby

MAIL CALL

One day I was to go on a simple mission for my 4 hours flight pay. This was a bomb sight check that only required a skeleton crew; a pilot, co-pilot, bombardier, flight engineer, and a photographer to record the findings. There was a new crew that had just arrived so the pilot from the new crew was sent as a co-pilot for this simple mission. There was a small island off the coast of Italy that was uninhabited. This island gave us a very good target for things like checking out bomb sights. It just happened that this mission had selected the Pied Piper, the plane I flew overseas on, as the plane we would use. We would use 3 100lb bombs each with only tail fuses just for good spotting. When we took off, I took the arming pins from the bombs so that they would be armed. When we got to our target the clouds had gathered and we couldn't see this tiny island. With this we returned to base for now. On the way back I just thought that maybe I should put the pin back in those bombs, so I did. It proved to be a good move as the bombs might have gone off. The engineers were putting a culvert at the end of the runway so a plane would be able to continue on into the wheat field if he couldn't stop because of a damaged hydraulic brake system. This required a ditch to be built deep enough for a 24 inch culvert. Would you believe that this new pilot undershot the runway by landing too quickly and hit right into this ditch. This broke off our right strut and sent us about 1000ft down the runway on our belly! It mashed the bombs and the floor upward. I grabbed the bars that held the ball turret in place and hung on with all my might and laid as close to the floor as I could. I'll bet my fingerprints would still be on that bar. My knuckles were white. When I felt the last lunge, I leaped out the waist window and hit the ground running as fast as I could. I was afraid of those bombs exploding or a fire. When I thought I was far enough away I looked back to see the rest of the crew rolling out of the top hatch trying to get away themselves. This was the end of "The Pied Piper." I had flown it on its first trip and also it's last. Guess the good Lord was with me once more. "The Pied Piper" ended up in the bone yard.

Uninhabited Island for Practice

The Pied Piper Goes to the Boneyard

BON NOVI, YUGOSLAVIA

On May 29th the target was Bon Novi, Yugoslavia, to hit the city as well as a concentration of German troops. For this reason we loaded the 20lb frags again. The mission was a success with not too much opposition.

Bombing Ploesti Refinery

The next day we were scheduled to head back to Ploesti for the 3rd time. I decided to stay back and rest up for the next trip. Maybe the volunteers can handle it. After all, they will have to handle it if I ever get my 50 missions in and go home. I did attend interrogation the next day and my volunteer photographers had done a good job. There was the usual smoke screen and it sounded like there was a lot of flak but not too many fighters and of course we had the P38's for escort. They did loose one airplane but that is better than we had done before at this target. I decided to go tomorrow as the group is headed to France.

Flak Hit

MONTPELINZA, FRANCE

There usually weren't as many fighters in that direction. The weather was so bad when we reached the coast of France that we had to turn back. I was hoping we would get credited for this mission and we did.

On June 5th, the complete 15th Air Force was sent to the railroad yards in Northern Italy to stop the Germans from getting supplies to their troops in Italy. The Germans had evacuated and there was no longer any resistance. This was the day, June 5th, that the allied troops WALKED into Rome.

Mission Briefing

MUNICH, GERMANY

On June 9th we went to Munich, Germany to hit the railroad yards there. They had a lot of 88T anti-aircraft guns shooting at us but again they were breaking a bit low due to our chaff. That's the tinsel like strips we threw out that I mentioned earlier.

The weather was bad all over Europe.

B24 headed for Bomb Mission

FERENZ, ITALY

The next day, June 10th, we went to Ferenz, Italy to the air field there. This was about the only airfield the Germans could use in this area. We were very successful and all returned to base. I didn't see how the Germans could stand much more of the pounding we were giving them.

The next mission is back to Munich but I decided not to go. My volunteers are doing a pretty good job. We only lost one plane on that mission and that plane ditched in the Adriatic. They were picked up by the Coast Guard so that was not too bad. I think I had 34 or 35 missions under my belt. That's a long way from 50 so it may take me awhile to get them all in.

Lt. Graves kept asking me to slow down my missions so I thought I would as things seemed to be getting rougher each day. I did want to get my 50 missions in and go home. More important, I did want to go home even if it is a little later. I knew I was safe on the ground.

KOBLENZ RAIL YARDS

The next mission was to return to the Koblenz Railroad yards and the refinery near by. I thought this might be a pretty rough mission so I decided I would sit it out. I went to interrogation and it sounded like I made a pretty good decision as the flak was intense but luckily was breaking low. That is due to the chaff the men threw out of the waist window like we had been doing for some time. There was only one plane missing when they returned but it sounded like from the men that were on that mission that they thought most of the crew got out ok.

Newer Silver B24

We got a couple of new planes that were silver and had a nose turret. Whenever they changed anything on the planes their nomenclature would change. Our "Pied Piper" was B24E. These new planes were B24H's. The nose turret turned so that the front gunner would have better range. The guns were still 50 caliber. I guess someone decided that it didn't do any good to paint them olive drab anymore as we were in the sky and not on the ground. Also, I suppose that a little bit of paint weighed something. Just that small amount might help this big machine get off the ground. I presumed all the new ones that came in would be like these new ones.

Koblenz Railyard

ISLE OF CAPRI

After you had flown so many missions the Army thought you needed some R & R to get away from all the stress and strain. The Isle of Capri was just off the coast of Naples, Italy. That was a good place for this to happen. I went with a bus load all across Italy to Naples where we boarded a boat for the two hour trip to the island which was just a tourist spot before the war. Some of us rented kayaks and had a ball rowing around the island. I remember the blue grottos the most. You could go inside these little caves along the coastline and once inside the cave everything was really blue. I had never seen the water that clear and beautiful. When we returned to Naples we were taken to Pompeii where we could view the ancient city that had been covered up by the hot lava from the eruption of Mt. Vesuvius thousands of years ago. What a sight. A trip like that would have cost a lot before the war. After the week was over we were bussed back to the grinds of war. When I returned Lt. Graves would take his turn. I would be there to take care of the flights and the pictures that were needed by our chiefs. Having 33 mission behind me and hearing that they were going to let some of the men go home with around 40 missions completed, I decided that while Lt. Graves was gone I might slip in the rest of my missions so I could go home.

Blue Grotto at the Isle of Capri

Flying Through Flak

ASPERITY, ITALY

This mission was to Asperity, Italy where there was a small refinery that the Germans were taking advantage of due to us disrupting their supply from Ploesti. This shouldn't have been a very long or difficult mission. I picked a plane that was flying in the hole in low left so I could get some really good pictures. The pilots name was Jim Corbett. They nicknamed him Gentlemen Jim because of the famous prize fighter by that name. Before we boarded the plane he called the crew together and gave a short prayer. That was great as I hadn't had any other pilot do this before. He did give me a bit of a scare though. We were still on the runway when we struck the steel mats on the other end. Usually the plane was in the air before we used that much runway. When we did take off you could tell he had plenty of flying speed to go up pretty quickly. The mission went well with no losses and after we landed I told Mr. Corbett that this is the first time anyone had used that much runway. He said, *"you see these guys crashing on take off, this isn't going to happen to me. I am going to have enough flying speed to counteract the downdraft caused by the other runway."* The mission was a great success and all planes returned to base. We only got credit for one mission compared to two if we went a long way out such as Vienna, Bucharest, Ploesti and others a long way from Italy.

PIACENZA, ITALY AIR DROME

We headed for the Piacenza Air Drome with 20lb frag bombs. These small bombs were used to damage airplanes on the ground and also personnel manning those fields. I never liked to fly in the hole when we carried those light bombs as they fly almost straight back once they leave the Bombay. I always tried to find out who was flying in #6 position so I wouldn't have to worry about one of those 20lbs bombs hitting our plane. This didn't happen in any of our missions but I always worried about there being a first time. The mission went well. There were some fighters but our P38's took care of them. All planes returned to base.

They were going to Chamberry, France the next day to hit the marshalling yard there. I thought I had better sit this one out. I was sure Lt. Graves would like that.

I was a Staff Sergeant and Lt. Graves told me that he was going to get me raised to Tech Sergeant as soon as he could because the head of the photo producing was a tech so he thought I should be the same because without staff, the photo producing staff was nothing.

I never stayed long enough to get that last promotion. I was wounded and came home. I really didn't care at this point if it meant I got to come home.

On June 25th, the 450th bomb group had a very bad day. I might note here that these planes had white tails. The crew of one plane had decided they wanted to get some Messerschmitts, so they pulled out of formation, feathered a couple props, which means they stopped a couple of engines, and lowered their landing gear. Lowering the landing gear was a means of letting the enemy know that you are surrendering. They got three Messerschmitt 109's to hover close to escort them back to a German air field and capture them. The Germans could use our planes after a surrender to radio our altitude to the guns below. We knew they had done this with a B17 out of England. As soon as the German 109's got in close the gunners of the B24 opened fire and got two of them! One got away. The B24 started it's engines, raised it's land gear and pulled back into formation. That night, Berlin Sally said on her radio program, *"All right you white tailed bombers...we will get you!"* It happened that my squadron had one half of our tails painted white, so I guess that is why we were on their list to get the next day...and they did. Their fighters were being depleted somewhat so they would try to throw all they had on the lead group to try and disrupt our timing.

LINZ, AUSTRIA

On July 28, 1944 our group, the 454th bomb group, had been selected to lead the entire 15th Air Force on a trip to Linz, Austria where the Herman Goring tank works were located along with other important plants building war machines for the German army. I might note again that our planes also had half white tails. Berlin Sally had said earlier, *"we'll get you white tailed bombers"*. They must have thought that it was us that shot down two of their 109s, because they sure came after us with a fury. We were leading the whole 15th Air Force and even though we had P38 fighters for cover, they were just like a swarm of bees flying around us. They threw all of their fire power at us. There was so much racket. Suddenly a 20mm shell from one of their fighters came right through the side of our plane, bursting on contact! A small piece hit me in the right arm and another one hitting me in the buttocks. A large one hit my right hand. I didn't realize how hard a bullet hit until this time. When I pulled my glove off, my trigger finger stayed in the glove! My middle finger was just hanging on by some skin. There was blood all over the place and it looked really bad. All I could do was start cussing at the Germans. I wasn't even mad at them until this time. We were all just doing our job. We paid the price for the maneuvers of the 450th. I say we, but so did I personally. Man, the adrenalin was pumping! I thought about how I wouldn't be able to pitch baseball anymore. (I did pitch a little after all of my wounds healed up). I tried to keep taking pictures. When the word got to the front of the plane that I had been hit, and we were away from the target and the fighters, the navigator came back to patch me up the best he could. There was some powdered penicillin in the first aid box so he just poured a lot of it on my hand and wrapped it with gauze. It didn't hurt too much as I let it freeze a bit to make it numb. When we reached our base someone in the crew shot off a red flare that told the ambulance to meet us. We had a wounded man aboard. When they loaded me in that ambulance I was rushed out of there. I did not get to go back to my tent and get my stuff. I lost everything. All I had was my flying coveralls that I had on. This is why I didn't get home with all of my pictures. Later my friend Pate sent me the ones that I have.

When we would leave briefings before going on bombing missions, we would be issued an escape packet in a 6" x 6" plastic box about 2 inches thick. It would just fit in the zipper pocket of our flying coveralls. In this packet was a digestible map of location of where you were going to be flying over so you might be able to figure out where you were should you get shot down. It also contained a small nutrition bar that was supposed to provide enough energy to last quite awhile. There was a fish hook and a very little compass and $50.00 in American marked money. This packet was all I had other than what I had on. It was in my knee pocket. On my way home I traded in the American money for lire in a poker game. Everyone wanted American money.

During this last mission that I flew, the Germans did lose a lot of their forces, but so did we and I don't know how many P38's we lost that day but I know our bomber losses were tremendous. I heard while in the hospital that we only had sixteen airplanes available to fly the next day. The rest had either been shot down or had been damaged so badly that they needed attention. Quite a few men including myself got hurt that day even though they got back to base. There was some damage to our airplane when I got hit. The automatic pilot controls to the tail had been shot in to and of course a big hole in the fuselage of our plane. I was still alive. I guess it wasn't my time.

BARI, ITALY HOSPITAL

When I was waiting for attention at the hospital they asked me if I could wait awhile as there were so many wounded soldiers to work on. Due to the fact that I wasn't having much pain I told them to go ahead and help the others. My hand started to thaw out a bit before they finally got to me. One of the things I remember that day was when the surgeon said to me, *"Son, I think I will sew your middle finger back on even in the shape it is in. They will probably have to take it off again but by then you will be back home."* When he said the word HOME, I was willing for him to do anything. Take my whole arm if necessary.

The next day I was laying on my hospital cot with my hand up as high as I could because it was hurting pretty bad.

A young medic came through the row of beds. I looked at him and decided he had to be a man from home. So as he passed by I said, *"Bill,"* and he turned around. Then I knew it was Bill Naylor from Macomb, Illinois. He had been a childhood playmate of my wife, Bette. He was stationed there as a medic and had a barracks close by. After a short talk, he asked me if there was anything he could do for me. I thought, yes, if he would write to Bette, since he knew her, and tell her that I would be ok, that would be a big help especially since I could not write. It happened that she got his letter one morning and that afternoon she got a telegram from the US government stating that I had been seriously injured in action. It surely did help her as the word "seriously" could have meant anything.

After I talked to Bill Naylor, I noticed another patient a couple of beds down from me and thought I recognized him from our outfit. I said, *"Aren't you from the 454th?"* and, he said, *"Yes, I got shot down with Lt. Sensor over Yugoslavia about a month ago."* I told him that Lt. Sensor brought that crippled airplane back to Italy. *"No,"* he said, *"we got shot down."* I told him that you guys in the back of the plane jumped out but the guys in the front got back. He argued with me for awhile and then began to believe that I was telling the truth. *"Will they court marshal us,"* he asked? I told him there was no problem because you were given the bells to jump and you did. He and the rest of the guys that jumped out got picked up by the Partisans. Partisans were a group of renegades that didn't go along with the German invasion but were not strong enough to resist it completely. If they picked up an American flier they would help him get home. There was another group called "The Chetnicks." They would also help Americans, but these 2 groups didn't get along. This is how he made it back.

I spent the next month there being treated for my wounds and recuperating. The stay at the hospital in Bari, Italy was long and tiring. I was recuperating from my wounds and I didn't feel needed by the Army. I thought that if I was going home we should just hurry up and get to it.

There wasn't much to do to occupy my time. We played poker in the day room almost all day. We would play a small stake game on a 20 lire limit. Usually 7 Card Stud was the game of choice. We would be awakened about 6am and told to get cleaned up for breakfast. There would be about an hour to waste so we would start the poker game. One morning after we had played for about 25 minutes a boy looked at his cards and said, "*I think this deck is crooked cause I have a three of clubs up and also a three of clubs down.*" We looked the deck over and it was really mixed up. We had been playing all that time and didn't even notice it. We had to find someone with two good hands to deal. It usually ended up that one person had to do all of the dealing. To change activities I would sometimes go out into the courtyard of the hospital and play horseshoes. I couldn't use my right hand, and soon got so I could pitch the horseshoes almost as good left-handed. Finally, I was ready to start my journey home.

C47 Transport

We were loaded onto a C-47 transport plane for Naples, Italy. It was a very light weight plane and as we were going over the mountains the turbulence was so bad that we were being tossed around. It made most of us sick, even though we were flight oriented soldiers. In Naples we were to catch a hospital ship home.

NAPLES, ITALY

When we got to Naples, we were taken to a Catholic hospital on a hill over looking the bay where the ships come in. This is where we were to wait to catch the hospital ship home. It so happens that this hospital ship was being used in the southern France invasion. We just had to wait. We spent about two weeks waiting with nothing to do but lay around on the roof and sun bathe. We would lay there with nothing on except maybe a towel. The nuns would come up on the roof and walk around. I guess that's how they got their thrill for the day.

Hospital Ship

Finally the invasion in France was over and the hospital ship came to pick us up for our trip home.

During the maneuvering near the southern coast of France the ship captain had gotten into the sand and bent the shaft that runs the prop. This caused us to come all the way across the Atlantic Ocean at 15 knots or less. We encountered a lot of rough waters which made the ship surge up and down a lot. Our bunks were down in the hold and it was pretty warm because the big engines were nearby. I would get a little seasick and the only way to get over this nausea was to go up on deck and watch the waves ahead. This sure made for a long trip. (After the war I used this tactic on my children when they became carsick. I would have them in the front seat and watch the road ahead so they would get accustomed to the rolling of the car).

In August I was on my home.

Romania had switched sides and joined with the US and our allies against Germany. The ranking Col. Gun was a prisoner of war in one of their camps. I learned later that a couple of days after I was wounded Col. Gun had talked one of the ME109 pilots into taking him back to the air strip at San Giovanni. The ME109 was a one seat plane so they packed him into the fuselage and painted a US flag on the side. They flew low into our air strip. There wasn't too much danger of being shot at by coming in low. Upon seeing the US flag on the plane our crews went to meet this plane. When Col. Gun climbed out of the fuselage it was quite a surprise. He then took some converted B17's that had bomb racks removed over to these stalag camps and brought all of the POW's back to San Giovanni 20 at a time. WOW!

CHARLESTON, SOUTH CAROLINA

We landed at the Port of Charleston in the middle of October. After we got settled we were allowed to go into town.

On the bus ride into town all of us were hollering at the pretty girls on the street. It was really noisy. After they let us off the bus downtown we all spread out and went mostly to local taverns. One of the convalescents had a body cast from his hip to his head holding his head back because he had a broken neck. During the night, he got some help to cut that cast off and went back to the base without it. That didn't set too well with the doctor, so needless to say, we were grounded from that time until we were sent to a hospital nearer our homes.

Hospital Ship Landing in South Carolina

INDIANAPOLIS, INDIANA

I went by train to Billings General Hospital in Indianapolis, Indiana. The first day there I spotted, Jack Jones, a man from Tennessee, Illinois. As it turned out he was going home the next day the same as I was so that was going to be great. It was good for him that he had a friend with him because he couldn't put his coat on without help. He had been shot in the shoulder and could not lift his arm at all. Jack was a drinker, and I did have a little problem with him because when our train was to leave he was in the tavern and I couldn't get him out in time to catch the train, so, we had to wait for the next one. When you are so anxious to get home, one more day can seem like forever. When we got to Galesburg, Illinois, the conductor said, *"Soldier, where do you want to get off? The train stops in Colchester and Augusta."* Jack said, *"I am getting off in Tennessee."* The conductor said, *" We don't stop there."* Jack replied in a very rough voice, *"We are this time, or I will hang on that brake rope all the way to Colmar!"* The Engineer finally agreed to stop in Tennessee and he told Jack that he would stop and let him off where he wanted.

HOME COLCHESTER, ILLINOIS

Bette and her mother, Edna, met me when the train arrived in Colchester. This was the only time that "Jake" the pet rooster did not come to meet me. We spent some time hashing over the situation before we went to Tennessee to see my parents, Peck and Annie. They were so very glad to see me. They had not seen me in nearly two years. Bette and I had stored our furniture in the attic of my parents three story house. We went upstairs to see how our furniture had faired the war. Everything looked the same as we had left it. I had ten days at home and the time went really fast. We had a lot of people to visit. After my leave was over I went back to Indianapolis. I do not remember what happened to Jack Jones but he didn't go back to Indiana with me. During my first visit with the doctor, he decided he would graft some skin from my leg onto my hand. Bette came out to the hospital with me for a few days. They put me to sleep with ether after painting and shaving my leg for the procedure. However, something changed their mind after they started and they decided not to make the graft. That is when I had the sickest day of my life. I am sure glad that they do not use ether today as it was really bad.

Group Getting Purple Heart

Next in Line for the PURPLE HEART

As soon as I finally got over the sickness from the ether, I just set around waiting orders.

Someone came to me and told me to go to a special room in the hospital. There was going to be a special ceremony for some men to receive medals. I was to be one of the recipients. There were 13 of us to be honored with Purple Hearts for being wounded in action. I was to receive in addition to the Purple Heart, the Distinguished Flying Cross for meritorious service.

The Distinguished Flying Cross is awarded to any person who, while serving in any capacity with the Armed Forces of the United States, distinguishes himself by heroism or extraordinary achievement while participating in aerial flight. The performance of the act of heroism must be evidenced by voluntary action above and beyond the call of duty. The extraordinary achievement must have resulted in an accomplishment so exceptional and outstanding as to clearly set the individual apart from his comrades or from other persons in similar circumstances. I didn't know at the time that I was to receive such a medal. I felt very honored.

HEADQUARTERS
FIFTEENTH AIR FORCE
APO　　520

20 August 1944

GENERAL ORDERS)
NUMBER 2690　　)　　　　　E X T R A C T

Award of the Distinguished Flying Cross.........................Section 1

SECTION I - Awards of the Distinguished Flying Cross.

Under the provisions of AR 600-45, as amended, and pursuant to authority contained in Circular No. 9, Hq MATOUSA, 10 July 1944, the Distinguished Flying Cross is awarded the following named personnel, Air Corps, United States Army, position, date of act and residence as indicated, with the following citation:

For extraordinary achievement while participating in aerial flight in the Mediterranean and North African Theatres of operations. Showing a high order of courage, leadership and professional skill, these gallant air crew members have distinguished themselves throughout many long and hazardous combat missions against the enemy despite severe and adverse weather conditions and enemy opposition by large numbers of fighters aircraft and intense, accurate and heavy anti-aircraft fire. Displaying great combat spirit and aggressiveness, these men have met, engaged and defeated the enemy regardless of the odds and in spite of the fact that at times their planes were so severely damaged that only by extraordinary skill and fortitude were they able to fight their way through to their objectives and aid in the grave damage inflicted upon the enemy. By their heroism, skill and airmanship, as shown throughout their combat careers, together with their intense devotion to duty during this period of intense combat operations against the enemy. These men have upheld the highest traditions of the military service, thereby reflecting great credit upon themselves and the Armed Forces of the United States of America.

＊ ＊ ＊ ＊ ＊ ＊ ＊ ＊ ＊ ＊ ＊ ＊ ＊ ＊ ＊ ＊ ＊ ＊

WAYNE W. WHITE, 16075918, Staff Sergeant, 739th Bomb Sq. 454th Bomb Group, Aerial Photographer, Austria 25 July 1944. Residence at Enlistment: Colchester, Ill.

By command of Major General TWINING:

R. K. TAYLOR
Colonel, GSC
Chief of Staff

OFFICIAL:

/s/ J. K. Ivins
J. K. IVINS
Colonel AGD
Adj General.

A TRUE EXTRACT COPY

ROLLIN L. PERRY
1st Lt. AGD

Distinguished Flying Cross

　　I guess the doctors thought that the best thing for my condition was just time. They said, *"why don't you just go home for ten more days and we will take a look at you when you return."* This seemed to be a pattern as I got at least 3 or 4 more leaves before I was discharged with a medical discharge. "Jake" the rooster would meet me every time I came home.

On June 28, 1945, I was handed $200.00, a disability discharge and a thank you for serving paper. That is it…. thank you for your time.

"JAKE the ROOSTER"

FACTS

During the summer of 1944 there were 1274 US prisoners of war in the Bucharest and Ploesti area.

The 15th Air Force consisted of 13 Bombardment Groups. All flew missions over Europe from the air bases in Italy.

During the 18 months that the 15th Air Force that was in operation there were 3544 B24's and 1407 B17's in Europe. 1756 B24's were lost and 624 B17's. In Ploesti alone 350 B24's were lost.

The 15th United States Air Force had crippled the enemy's transportation system over half of once occupied Europe with repeated fighter and bomber attacks. The 15th dropped 303,842 tons of bombs on enemy targets in 12 countries in Europe.

The 454th Bombardment Group, flying from Italy flew 243 missions on over 150 primary targets in Italy, Yugoslavia, Austria, Bulgaria, Hungary, Romania, France, Germany, Czechoslovakia, Greece, and Poland. During this time, the 454th dropped 13,389 tons of bombs on enemy marshalling yards, oil refineries, bridges, installations, airdromes, and rail lines.

My Bombardment Group started with 4 photographers and 16 volunteers. I was the only one left of the original 4 and when I was sent home there were only 3 left of the volunteers! It really wasn't my time.

Purple Heart - Distinguished Flying Cross - Air Medal

WWII Memorial

WWII Memorial USAAF Liberators

POST SCRIPT

The WWII Veterans are the men and women who survived a long war and many hard battles. In their honor, and the honor of those who didn't survive, a grateful nation, the United States of America, built a Memorial in Washington.

I was so very honored to be a part of the recent Honor Freedom Flight to Washington with 33 of my fellow veterans.

One of them was 97 years old. I looked at these men, some in wheelchairs, and it is hard to tell that once they were young soldiers that went to fight for a great cause. After they won the war they hung up their weapons as monuments, and returned quickly to civilian life and prospered as free men should.

We left from Hannibal, Missouri during the night and were taken by bus to St. Louis, Missouri, where we boarded a plane for Baltimore.

I have to tell you that I thought it was just going to be a flight of a bunch of old men to see the WWII Memorial in Washington.

I was so wrong!

I was so surprised that they would also honor us at security by not making the WWII vets remove their shoes and go through the normal security. They must have realized that we were no threat to our country.

When we landed in Baltimore there were over 200 strangers, waving flags, hugging us, and shaking our hands. Thanking us for our service. We were all emotionally affected by such a tender moment.

Then we boarded a bus and went to the Memorials.

Words just cannot express the feeling and emotion that comes over you when you see such magnificent tributes to the men and women who have fought for our country.

We visited the Arlington Cemetery and watched the changing of the guard at the Tomb of the Unknown Soldier. It was just breath taking to see the rows of white tombstones. Visiting the Memorials in Washington truly revitalizes your American spirit.

After visiting all of the war memorials we started our journey home.

When we boarded the bus in St. Louis to return to Hannibal, there were over 40 Harley Davidsons lined up in front of our bus giving us an escort back.

They are called the Patriot Guard which is made up of vets of more recent wars with huge flags on each cycle. They go as escorts to see fallen soldiers home, they attend funeral processions and special military events to show respect for the deceased.

Watching their masses riding in a procession with their lights and flags was truly a spectacular sight. We had traffic backed up for miles.

As we stepped off the bus our names were called off with our military branch and a salute. Then we were greeted by our families and again hundreds of people waving huge flags.

After this trip I felt the need to do more. I decided to put my stories and feelings in print in an effort to let everyone know that all American soldiers have left a legacy of freedom, and they have taught us the value of sacrifice, the conditions of freedom, and the love of country.

MANY YEARS LATER

After World War II, my wife and I raised three children. We had a prosperous and interesting life. I lost my wife, Bette, in 1995.

Over the years I kept in touch with my crew members that survived. Now, the only one living is Norbit Rudy and myself. My partner in life is Nancy Aydelotte. She is the widow of the 454th Bombardment Group Gunner, Don Aydelotte. Life is good. It still isn't my time.

Wayne White & Nancy Aydelotte

Author

Wayne W. White

In this book, Wayne White recalls his experiences as a B24 Photographer during World War II. In 1943, at age 20, White left his hometown in Illinois and began flying bombing missions with the 454th Bombardment Group, US 15th Air Force. He learned first hand the terror and fear of war.

Based in Italy the Fifteenth Army Air Force flew bombing raids over Europe. The Fifteenth Air Force was instrumental in destroying the German transportation system and oil supply.

White reflects on the 37 missions he flew as well as great personal stories of what life was like for him at this time.

The odds were against him ever surviving. The losses he witnessed made him believe that it just wasn't his time.